5

Copyright © 1988 by Michael Neugebauer Verlag AG, Gossau Zürich, Switzerland.
First published in Switzerland under the title Das Löwen-Kinder-Buch
English translation copyright © 1988 by Patricia Crampton

Originally published in the United States, Canada, Great Britain, Australia, and New Zealand
by Picture Book Studio Ltd. Reissued in paperback in 1995 by North-South Books, an imprint
of Nord-Süd Verlag, AG.

Distributed in the United States by North-South Books Inc., New York.

Library of Congress Cataloging-in-Publication Data
Hofer, Angelika
The Lion Family Book.
Translation of: Das Löwen-Kinder-Buch.
Summary: Text and photographs take the reader into a family of lions to watch
the cubs grow and learn on the African plains.
1. Lions—juvenile literature. [1. Lions] I. Ziesler, Günter, ill. II. Title.
QL737.c23H61613 1988 599.74'428 88-15139

A CIP catalogue record for this book is available from The British Library.

ISBN 1-55858-502-8 (paperback) 10 9 8 7 6 5 4 3 2 1
Printed in Italy

Ask your bookseller for these other North-South Animal Family books:
THE CROCODILE FAMILY BOOK by Mark Deeble and Victoria Stone
THE GRIZZLY BEAR FAMILY BOOK by Michio Hoshino
THE PENGUIN FAMILY BOOK by Lauritz Somme and Sybille Kalas

Angelika Hofer
Günter Ziesler

The Lion Family Book

Translated by
Patricia Crampton

A MICHAEL NEUGEBAUER BOOK
NORTH-SOUTH BOOKS / NEW YORK / LONDON

Deep in the central plains of far-off Africa, we are going to visit "the land of the great herds."

Its inhabitants, the Masai, call it "Mara" – "speckled land." The colored specks on the grassy plains are acacia trees, zebras, gnus, antelopes and gazelles.

Buried in the soft hilly landscape of the plains, rivers bordered by thick forest seek out a passage. They are the lifeblood of this land, carrying its vital supplies of food and water.

Where the great herds graze, predators live too: hyenas, wild dogs, leopards and cheetahs, and the "King of the Beasts," the lion. We are going to find out more about this great hunter, so much admired by human beings for his beauty, strength and courage. His coat is the color of the golden-yellow grass, the color of Africa.

My name is Angelika. I spent a year living with Günter in the "Masai Mara" Nature Reserve, to study and photograph the animal world of Africa.
This VW Campingbus is our home and mobile blind from which we can observe the animals without disturbing them.
Our campsite is in the forest by the river, the only place where we can move a few yards away from the car without being in danger.

It is still early in the morning. Two splendid male lions are lying in the dew-soaked grass by the Musiara Swamp. We have given them African names: Momba and Meru.

Momba and Meru greet the new day with loud roars, their deep voices rolling across the plain. All the animals listen.

These four lionesses are also listening intently. They are the wives of Momba and Meru and we have named them Talek, Tara, Miti, and Ola.

Lions live in large family groups, known as prides. In the vastness of the plains every pride lays claim to an area of many square miles, so the members of the family have to roar loudly to keep in touch. They tell each other where they are, and inform neighboring prides: "This is our kingdom. No strange lions allowed here!"

Around noon the rays of the sun strike the earth almost vertically, because the land of the great herds lies on the equator. Even in winter it is still warm and summery here.

Talek, Tara, Miti, Ola, and their six one-year-old cubs sleep through the heat of the day in the shade of an acacia. Just like house cats on a hot day, they lie with all four paws outstretched, completely relaxed.

In the cool of the evening it is time for the lions to get up. For them evening turns into morning and night into day. They yawn and stretch, clean their coats with their rough tongues and lick each others' faces. Gradually the whole pride wakes up. When darkness falls the lions set off across the plains in small groups.

Only Talek steals away on her own. Do you see how round her tummy is? She will be bringing her babies into the world tonight. She will find a hiding-place for them somewhere in the high grass or in the undergrowth. A safe place is vital for the lion cubs because the lioness often leaves them alone for hours while she goes hunting. At such times the blind, helpless cubs could easily be taken by hyenas, leopards, or birds of prey.

We are in luck! After searching for weeks we have at last found the lion nursery among the withered branches of a fallen tree. Talek is taking good care of her young.

The babies are already almost a month old, as big as full-grown house cats, and their eyes are open. But the cubs will not be able to walk steadily for a few weeks yet.

On our trips we often visit the nursery and watch as the cubs come out of their hiding-place to play in the warm morning sunshine.

This is Simba, Talek's little son. When he is three years old and his mane begins to grow, he will leave the pride and spend a few years roaming across the plains. During this time he will mature into a full-grown lion, with a splendid mane to protect him in battles with rivals. One day he will have a pride of his own, while his sisters stay on in their mother's pride – but all this is still in the future. For now, Simba and his sisters only want to play.

Playing makes them hungry. The babies mew and whimper until the lioness rolls on her back and allows them to drink. As soon as they are satisfied the cubs fall asleep, one by one.

One morning we meet Talek on the road with her cubs. The baby lions are two months old now and so steady on their feet that they can follow their mother to the pride. Talek urges the cubs on with soft grunts, but they are much more interested in their games.

Talek grows impatient, grabs one of her babies by the scruff of the neck and walks on. But before she has gone far, Simba discovers that the tuft of her tail makes a good toy. Simba's teeth are sharp! Talek drops the cub she is carrying and hisses at her mischievous son.

On the way to the pride Talek meets her sister Tara, who now also has two babies of the same age.

Tara and Talek hiss at each other, nervous at this first meeting in the company of their cubs. But this anxiety will soon be forgotten and the mother lions will share their maternal duties.

When one lioness goes hunting, the other will take care of the babies and even let them suckle as if they were her own.

Within the pride the lion cubs are brought up in safety. In their play they develop friendships amongst themselves and with the other members of the pride.

Simba has found a big brother and tries to rub cheeks with him, as cats do. But look what big brother does! He uses the baby's back as a convenient resting place for his heavy head.

The young lions are learning the rules of living together in the pride.
The language of lions is not very different from the language of house cats.
When he growls and hisses, the lion is saying: "I don't like you, stay away
from me." And when a lion shows his teeth it means: "I've had enough!
Leave me in peace!" And that goes for Simba, too.

At sunset the lionesses set off for the hunt. They prefer to hunt together and under cover of darkness.

This means that the grass-eaters – the zebras, gnus, antelopes, and gazelles – have to be particularly alert at night. Several animals in the herd always stand guard, like this topi antelope.

Lions can run fast, but not for very long. They could never chase their prey over long distances like the swift, slender cheetah. That is why lions drive the prey towards each other, hunting as a team. This enables them to kill animals which are larger, heavier, and, above all, faster than they are. The females, with their slimmer bodies, are the most skillful hunters, and because they have no mane, it is easier for them to stay hidden. That is why it is usually the lionesses who bring in the food for the pride.

Last night they were successful again, and as day dawns Talek leads her cubs to the prey.

The lionesses have killed a gnu and eaten most of it themselves, but now it is the cubs' turn. Only when the lionesses have had enough meat will there be something left over for the young lions.

So even a mother lion thinks of herself first. It seems selfish, but think about it: How can the pride survive unless the hunters and defenders of the area are strong and well-fed? It was obviously a delicious meal!

There is no winter in Africa. The "small rains" in November are followed by the "dry time." Rain and thunder clouds will not darken the sky again until March, April, and May. The Africans say: "Now is the time of the great rains." Later the sun will burn down again every day from a cloudless sky. Then the Africans will say "the great dry time" is beginning.

Huge herds of gnu are on the move all the year round, in search of fresh grass and water. In September they cross the border from the Serengeti in Tanzania to the Masai Mara in Kenya. Where the grass still rippled on the plain a short time ago, there are now countless black dots on a golden-yellow background: gnus, gnus, and more gnus, as far as the eye can reach. They pour down the slopes in long lines which meet in a broad stream, and on the plains they gather in their thousands, like a great, dark sea.

Now Simba and the other lion cubs are nearly a year old. Full of youthful high spirits, they have begun to play at hunting.

They lie in wait for each other in the lee of a hillside, just as they will lie in wait for their prey. They chase each other, just as they will chase their prey. When one overtakes another he lashes out at his playmate with one paw, just as he will lash out at his prey.
For the time being it is all a game, in which anyone can be either hunter or hunted; but one day the game will be played in earnest.

As long as herds of gnu populate the Mara in huge numbers the lions find it worthwhile to hunt by day as well.

They know that zebras and gnus go down to the water every morning, so they steal through the grass and lie in wait by the wateringplace.

But zebras and gnus are always alert. They sniff the air rapidly: Did one of them catch the scent of lion? They watch suspiciously for the slightest movement. So many eyes, ears, and noses – a lioness must be both skilled and cautious, or she is sure to be found out.

The cubs watch their mothers closely, seeing how lions work together in the hunt, learning how to stalk and how to make the kill.

But they are still too young to take part.

Suddenly Talek springs from cover and races after a gnu. The rest of the herd scatters in panic. Somewhere in the high grass Ola is waiting and Talek drives the gnu towards her.

Ola bursts from her hiding-place like a coiled spring and pulls the prey down with her paws. The gnu dies quickly as Ola's teeth meet in its throat.

Talek and the cubs run up, hoping to get enough food for themselves before the others arrive.

Momba has been watching the hunt from a distance, though as a male lion he seldom takes part.

The leader of the pride has more important things to do: He has to make sure that no strange lions trespass on his family's hunting ground.

All the members of the family give way as Momba strides towards the kill to secure his share. Only vultures and marabous sit and wait until he has eaten his fill. They are the garbage-men of the plains, and remove everything that is left: bones, skin, and entrails.

Everyone is well-fed and contented. No more disputes over the prey, nothing but sleepy well-being. The lions sleep through the rest of the day in the shade of a tree.

In October the great herds move on.
We too must say good-bye to our lion family and to the Masai Mara.
As darkness falls, we listen for the last time to the lions roaring their
message across the vastness of the grassy plains. The Africans know
what the lions are saying:

"Hii nchi ya nani? Hii nchi ya nani?
  Yango, Yango, Yango."
"Whose is this land? Whose is this land?
  It is ours—ours—ours . . ."